Stand Your Ground

How to Cope with a Dysfunctional Family
and Recover from Trauma

Katherine Mayfield

Stand Your Ground. Copyright © 2016 by Katherine Mayfield.

ISBN # 9780997612110
Second Edition published by The Essential Word Press.

Disclaimer: This book is not intended to be a substitute for professional counseling or medical assistance. Readers are advised to seek medical attention or psychiatric help if the situation warrants professional or medical advice.

Also by Katherine Mayfield

*Bullied: Why You Feel Bad Inside and
What to Do About It*

The Box of Daughter

*Dysfunctional Families: Exposing the Secrets
Behind Closed Doors*

*Dysfunctional Families: Healing the Legacy
of Toxic Parents*

The Box of Daughter and Other Poems

The Meandering Muse

*What's Your Story?: A Quick Guide
to Writing Your Memoir*

Praise for Katherine Mayfield's Work

"...A testament to the merit of psychological healing through the understanding and expression of feelings."
—Kirkus Reviews

"Katherine Mayfield holds nothing back, and her unflinching, thorough, and articulate honesty is a true gift for anyone wanting to understand, face, and rise above the emotional scars of a damaging childhood."
—Amy Wood, Psy.D., author of *Life Your Way*

"Well-written, intriguing, and so very enlightening!"
—LibraryThing

"Fresh, bold, and inspiring."
—Examiner.com

"A compelling and insightful expose of the damage bullying can do to a child's self-esteem, and of measures that can be taken to stop it....For anyone who ever found themselves at the mercy of a bully, Mayfield's latest offering is definitely a book to have front and center on your shelves."
—*Nashua Telegraph*

Contents

Stand Your Ground

How to Cope with a Dysfunctional Family
and Recover from Trauma

Introduction

Growing up in a dysfunctional family can create all kinds of difficulties in our lives, from subtle codependence to post-traumatic stress disorder, and everything in between. Dysfunctional families range along a continuum from slightly maladjusted to severely dysfunctional, depending on the interactions and behaviors of the family members.

Here are some indicators that a family is not functioning in a way that supports each family member. The more of these indicators you can identify in your family, the more dysfunctional your family probably is.

1. Some family members are overly critical of others without providing positive feedback and support.

2. New ideas are usually belittled and/or scoffed at.

3. There is a strong sense of "drama," meaning that small problems or mistakes are blown up into momentous dramatic complications. At the same time, family members are sometimes afraid to explore, try new things, and/or live a fuller life. (See Chapter 2 for information on the "Drama Addiction.")

4. Each member of the family seems to have a designated "role"—whether they like it or not—such as the peacemaker, the boss, the complainer, the achiever, the underdog, the rebel, the outsider.

5. Some members in the family are generally the "givers," and others are generally "takers."

6. Choosing to do something outside of the family "norm" is frowned upon.

7. Family "rules" are rigid, and there is generally no opportunity to discuss them or take action to change them.

8. There are secrets in the family—whether between certain family members or among the entire group—that have shame attached to them. These secrets are never talked about, and efforts to bring them up for discussion in order to "clear the air" usually result in hitting a wall.

9. Shame and guilt are weapons used freely by people who manipulate others.

10. Family gatherings are often tense and stressful, rather than happy and fun or relaxed and enjoyable.

Even functional families probably exhibit some of these circumstances once in awhile, but in a dysfunctional family, they occur frequently, and are as inflexible and unchangeable as a post buried in cement.

Life is fluid, and changes from day to day, week to week, year to year. People also grow and change, and need room to explore and develop their potential. When the dynamics of a dysfunctional family remain static and unchanging, the individual members of that family will have difficulty making positive changes and moving forward in their lives if they're not working to overcome the negative beliefs and ingrained behavior patterns.

This guide is meant to help you understand more clearly how any dysfunctional patterns in your particular family affect your worldview and the way you cope with life, and to help you begin to recover from the difficulties that you experienced growing up so you can start moving forward and creating a better life for yourself based on who you are inside rather than as a byproduct of the patterns and beliefs you grew up with.

The first chapter will lay some groundwork, which will help you see your family patterns with more clarity and gain more understanding of unhealthy behaviors and beliefs that might be part of your experience with your family.

Later chapters will offer more insight and tips for coping with difficult family members, along with a simple system you can use to manage your feelings and recover from criticism, and exercises to help you work on problem areas.

Have compassion for yourself as you work with the ideas in this book. Most of us are taught to have compassion for others, but we're not often taught that we deserve it as much as anyone else. Allow yourself the space to feel what you feel, to see what you see, to believe what you believe, no matter what you were taught or what others say. Truth is not always comfortable, but it is the starting gate of healing.

And don't judge yourself for what you feel or think. Most of us were taught that what we feel and think is wrong, and society often encourages that view. But this is erroneous. Everyone has a right to their own opinions, thoughts, and feelings, no matter how much they may differ from others'.

No one has walked through life in your shoes, or experienced life as you have experienced it. Each of us is unique, with a unique viewpoint about life and relationships. Have as much respect for yourself and for your needs and viewpoints as you would for someone else. Though you may never have learned this, you do deserve as much good as everyone else, and you deserve as much compassion, love, and respect as everyone else.

Be gentle with yourself as you read through the book, and allow yourself to take the time you need with the process.

Journaling

Journaling is an extremely useful tool for getting to the root of issues and releasing feelings. Even if you don't think you're a "writer," I strongly encourage you to keep a journal as you go through this book. Don't worry about whether the spelling or sentence structure is correct, or whether you're using the right words. Just paint your thoughts and feelings onto the paper without criticizing yourself.

As you read, you may discover some insights about your family and the ways in which you relate with them, and if you don't record your insights, they can get fuzzy in your mind and slip back into unconsciousness, causing you to fall back into the old patterns. It helps in your recovery to have something written that you can refer back to—and the very act of writing itself will imprint the new insight more deeply on your mind.

A journal also helps you to release deep feelings by getting them out of your mind and onto paper. You can express everything you feel in a journal when you can't express it to the person who mistreated you. You can allow your anger or sadness to flow out in your writing, so it's no longer pent up in your mind and body. Journaling helps the free flow of feelings, which in time will allow you to let go of the past.

Even if, for safety reasons, you decide to discard each bit of writing, journaling will help you heal.

If you need more help

In some families, it's extremely painful much of the time to interact with certain family members. Sometimes it's so stressful to be with them that we have trouble coping with other areas of our lives. Though it may feel "normal" to you if you're in this situation, this is not the way we were meant to live, and it indicates that your family is probably very dysfunctional.

If your family creates so much distress in your life and relationships that you consistently feel angry, confused, hurt, or anxious, or have trouble focusing on other areas of your life, therapy is highly recommended. A therapist can give you emotional support, reality checks on your situation, and more tools for coping with dysfunctional family members. If working with a therapist is not possible, support groups are the next best thing. There are quite a few on the internet if you would prefer to remain anonymous. The important thing is to get some kind of support for yourself.

If there are no other options, try to find a friend, teacher, minister, or other person who you can talk with about the situation. Breaking the "rule of silence" in dysfunctional families is the first step toward true healing and creating an authentic life that works for you.

I've been where you are, smack in the middle of chaos and angst. Life can and does get better when you let yourself see the truth of the situation, take better care of yourself, and learn how to set some boundaries with your family (even if you're the only one that knows about them), such as spending less time with certain family members, or standing up to criticism.

As you gain self-esteem and more of a feeling of control over your life, the chaos will begin to fade into the background, and as you let it go, you'll free up all kinds of energy to be more proactive in creating a life that works for you.

I hope this book is helpful for you, and I wish you all the best on your journey!

Chapter 1: Digging Down to Find the Truth

What is "Spider Love"?

The form of "love" that many dysfunctional families embrace is actually more like "Spider Love," as Martha Beck called it in her wonderful book, *Steering by Starlight*. This kind of love sucks family members dry rather than nourishing them, wrapping them in webs of enmeshment and controlling them by creating guilt. "If you loved me, you would do this" is a good example.

Many families have an overall atmosphere of criticism and judgment, and sometimes parents criticize their kids and adult children in an attempt to help them become better people. But there's a big difference between offering comments that help a person to understand that there could be a better way of doing things, and repeated criticism that cuts self-esteem down to zero.

When people need you to "be like them," to do things their way instead of yours, or to pay attention to them without receiving attention and respect in return, this is "Spider Love." It creates a very unhealthy atmosphere in a family, and keeps family members from building self-esteem and becoming authentic (which means acting from their own core beliefs and creating what they as individuals want in life).

Real love in families is nourishing, encouraging all family members and helping them to grow and become the very best they can be. Real love offers give-and-take—at different times, everyone gives, and everyone receives—and real love includes compassion for difficulties someone is going through. If the love in your family feels more like "Spider Love," you might want to consider cutting down on the time you spend with your family, and creating loving, nourishing friendships and relationships instead.

Controlling behavior and manipulation in families

Dysfunctional families often have rigid ways of believing, behaving, and responding to life. When a child grows up in such a family, parents may control his or her behavior in any number of ways, causing inhibited development of the child's sense of self, and sometimes an impaired ability to make decisions.

Some parents even tell their children, "You don't feel that way," or "That's not the right way to think." These are attempts to encourage the child to behave in certain ways which are comfortable for parents to cope with rather than allowing a natural expression of the child's self. This kind of "controlling" does not encourage development of an authentic way of being

Children receive all kinds of messages from their parents, both verbal and nonverbal. Some parents control by using facial expressions or body language to indicate disapproval (what some children call "The Look"); some use words or physical actions.

Both verbal and nonverbal messages can be confusing and sometimes frightening, and over time will likely produce uncertainty in the child as to the validity of his or her own perceptions of life if he or she is not allowed the freedom of self-expression at the same time.

Children don't know enough about life and the world to question what a parent tells them, so they question themselves instead, and learn to mistrust their thoughts, feelings, and intuition. Then when they become adults, they have a hard time trusting themselves to make decisions that benefit them.

Sometimes they also have a hard time facing life, because they may tend to build a life that would suit their parents rather than a life that suits their innermost self, or continue to live by parental rules that they still don't understand, and then find they're unhappy with the life they've built.

If a child grows to adulthood without examining the view of life, self, and the world he or she grew up with, it's likely that quite a bit of this early "programming" will still affect the adult's opinion of self and the way in which he or she sees and interacts with the world. This can sometimes place limitations on how well the person copes with life and what they can accomplish.

When someone accepts their parents' worldview as "the only one" at an early age, he or she creates a version of reality based on the way the parent(s) saw life and the world. And since each person is unique, trying to use someone else's view of the world in life creates problems, misunderstandings, and failures because the person is not operating from their own authentic way of being.

Recovering from a dysfunctional childhood and developing an individual worldview and a more authentic way of living results from the process of examining our thoughts, feelings, behaviors, and beliefs, so that we can begin to understand how dysfunctional family dynamics may have encouraged us to develop in unhealthy ways, uncover the harmful messages we received, and create a new perspective about ourselves and our lives that works well for us. We begin to learn to trust ourselves and our own perspective, instead of those who might not be worthy of our trust.

Trust issues are not entirely about trusting other people. If we learned early on that we can't trust ourselves, we'll have a hard time trusting others. If you think this is true for you, pay some attention over the next few weeks to how many *good decisions* you make, and be sure to notice how many things you do right (cooking a meal? driving a car? doing your job? getting up on time? taking a shower?). Like most adults, you're probably pretty competent in most areas of your life; you've just been brought up to feel inordinately badly about any small misstep.

In dysfunctional families, people overfocus on problems—even very small ones—without allowing any focus on the innumerable ways a child does things well. This is one of the primary causes of low self-esteem. A child can do ten, fifty, a hundred things right in a day, but an overly critical parent will pick out the one thing that doesn't go well, and harp on it over and over.

In some families, the habit of criticizing *appears* to indicate that an individual who's being criticized doesn't do very well in life. But the criticisms may not always be grounded in reality. Some people just need to complain; some people criticize because it makes them feel like they don't have any problems themselves. By criticizing others, they're distracting themselves from working on their own issues, and making themselves feel more powerful by making someone else feel smaller.

If some members of your family are very critical of you, and you feel like you can't do anything right, maybe it's time to rethink the situation. Are all of their criticisms valid, or are they just looking for things to complain about, and you happen to be handy? When they criticize, do they *generalize*, as in "You always..." or "You never..."

The question to ask yourself is, Do you always or never do that? Or is it only once in a while? One of the favorite tricks of family bullies is to make criticisms global (blowing them out of proportion) so they seem much more important. Another favorite manipulation is to place a label on you, as in "Too bad you're not a better mother." How would someone know, since they don't see how you are with your kids day in and day out— only on special occasions?

Sometimes family bullies even make things up just so they can enjoy the feeling of power that the bullying gives them. If you notice yourself falling into guilt or despair when a criticism hits you, ask yourself, "Is that true?" If it's not, allow yourself to ignore it. If it is, ask yourself "To what degree?" Maybe you only did that on one occasion.

Keep digging inside to find the truth. You won't find it outside of yourself, only within. It's time to begin to trust your own perceptions and feelings, and to act on them with as much determination as you can muster.

The false self

Children who grow up in very controlling families often develop a "false self"—a constellation of behaviors that are not authentic to the child's inner self, but which are acceptable within the family, and thus keep the child feeling "safe."

Behaviors of the false self can include trying to please the parents, shutting down normal feelings such as anger, sadness, and fear, doing things in uncomfortable ways so as not to make waves, and playing certain roles in order to gain a sense of fitting in.

What happens as a child grows is that the development of the potential within the child is discarded in favor of the safer false beliefs and behaviors, so that even as an adult, such children may continue to act out the behaviors of the false self, sometimes without even being aware of it.

Here are some questions to help you find out whether you might be making life choices based on the false self rather than your own true needs and desires.

1. Do you sometimes wonder after you do something why you did it?

2. Do you often have trouble making decisions—as if there are always two (or more) parts of you wanting different things?

3. Have you ever made a choice, only to discover down the road that it wasn't really what you wanted?

4. Do you feel able to let others know when you need something?

5. Is it easy, difficult, or impossible for you to ask for help when you need it?

6. Are you in a job, relationship, or other situation that feels like it's not a good "match" for who you are?

7. Are you able to work toward achieving your deepest dreams and desires, even if you're going slowly?

8. Do you feel like your life is in your hands, or in someone else's?

Any "yes" answers indicates that you may have learned certain behaviors early on in order to fit in in your family, but they may no longer be serving you as an adult. While you're thinking about this idea, you might write a little in your journal about which parts of your life feel like they're "really you," and which feel like they don't really fit who you are inside. Making a drawing is also helpful in gaining clarity.

Now here are some questions to get you started on connecting with the authentic self inside of you.

1. If all of your time was your own, and you could choose what to do with your hours and days, what are some of the things you'd like to do?

2. Are there people you spend time with that you would like to leave forever?

3. Would you like to socialize more in your life? Less?

4. If you could have any job you wanted, what would it be?

5. If you could dress any way you wanted, what would that be?

6. Do you have a dream of who you really are inside? If so, what is it, and how would that self express itself? How would that self live your life?

7. If you could do anything you wanted to right now, what would it be?

Family secrets

What is most important to understand about dysfunctional families is that in keeping the family "secrets," we are harming ourselves and diminishing our ability to be honest and open-hearted with ourselves and others we care about (members of the family, significant others, or friends that we're close to).

Sometimes we even keep secrets from ourselves. We might have had insights flashing through our minds when we were young, or clarity about what was really going on in a situation, but we quickly repressed these thoughts because they were too uncomfortable to live with consciously, and we didn't know at a young age what to do with that knowledge.

Many people who grew up in dysfunctional families knew on some level that something about the atmosphere of the family was "wrong," but most never found validation for those feelings, so they just ignored their intuition.

Talking with people you trust about some of the issues in your family can give you tremendous validation for your feelings and your own view of what's going on within the family, and can help you to gain new understanding. "Reality checks" are an extremely important tool for people who struggle with dysfunctional family dynamics.

By seeking an objective view of the situation, you're helping yourself gain clarity about what's really going on under the surface. A therapist, minister, support group, or trusted friend can be a good sounding board—and in spite of how other people appear—happy, well-adjusted, together—most people do have some kind of difficulty with their families, so you're not alone in feeling uncomfortable in your family. You don't need to be ashamed to talk about your feelings.

In fact, most people in dysfunctional families were brought up to pretend that they're happy, and that everything's fine, so you can't ever truly know what's going on in someone else's life by looking at how they present themselves in public. With more than 90,000 therapists in the U.S. alone, it's pretty clear that a lot of people have issues they need help with!

If you have siblings who are open to discussing the situation without criticism or blame, you may be able to not only offer each other validation, but help each other discover a new perspective on the situation. But if any part of you fears that there would be some kind of retaliation, or that a sibling might not keep your words confidential, find someone else to talk with.

Learning to trust yourself

The discovery that some of the behaviors in your family that you thought and felt were wrong or abnormal actually *were* abnormal is tremendously freeing and validating, and helps you learn to trust yourself. Don't be afraid to ask if something seems normal to someone else. Even though dysfunctional family dynamics are usually well-hidden behind the closed doors of many families, almost everyone experiences them. We're just taught to "hide the family secrets," so we don't know that the same kinds of situations happen to other people. But they do.

Shedding light on the secrets and getting reality checks helps us ferret out the messages that caused us to create certain behaviors in expectation of certain results (i.e., being a people-pleaser in the hope that we would be loved)—behaviors that don't necessarily get us what we want or make us successful in the larger world as adults.

The first step in recognizing and recovering from dysfunctional family patterns is trusting your own instincts. Only you know what is true for you.

Children in dysfunctional families are often told, either verbally or nonverbally (through behavior, facial expressions, and/or role-modeling) that they're incapable of figuring things out for themselves, that their thoughts or opinions don't matter or aren't valid, or even that they're doing everything wrong and don't know anything.

Sometimes, in order to control their children and meet their own needs, parents will act as if they themselves are perfect in every way and always right about everything—which means that anyone else's view or way of doing things is always "wrong." This isn't necessarily true. But a child has no way to understand that no one is perfect, that their parents are creating a facade about who they are, and that their behavior may in fact be very dysfunctional in spite of appearances to the contrary.

Every person has a unique way of viewing the world, of coping with life—and what works for someone else might not work for you. You need to begin trusting your own viewpoints, your own intuition, your own beliefs. This is the only way you can create a life of your own, a more authentic life that's not based on the ingrained patterns of how your family reacts and responds.

You may find that some family members still belittle and criticize you as if what you're doing is wrong, but over time, if you hold to your own beliefs about what is really true, you'll raise your self-esteem and confidence. It may turn out, as it has for so many people, that you were right all along, and that you really can see the truth behind a dysfunctional family pattern.

Chapter 2: Coping with Repetitive Criticism

Criticism is a habitual, repetitive behavior in some families—parents may criticize everything from their children's choice of dress and their choice of friends to their opinions, beliefs, and ideas.

Recurring criticism wears down a child's sense of self and self-esteem, sometimes to the point where the child may feel quite helpless, as if nothing he or she does is right.

Many children of dysfunctional families carry this feeling into adulthood and feel like they can never do anything right. Often, these people are actually very capable and competent, but just aren't able to see themselves that way because of the messages they received.

Sometimes people criticize others repeatedly because it makes them feel powerful and "perfect." For others, it's simply the way they grew up themselves, and they don't know another way to interact with family members.

Criticism is really nothing but one person's opinion raised to the level of "the way it is." It's designed to control, either through making the criticized person conform, or by making them feel guilty or ashamed.

You don't have to believe in the criticism—you always have a choice; you always have free will. Realize that the person criticizing may not even be wanting to help you. They may just be feeling a little unsure in the moment, and by criticizing someone else, they help themselves feel more worthy.

People who've been repeatedly criticized often have a knee-jerk response to being criticized: we immediately take the criticism in and perceive it to be true, simply because it comes from outside. But if you take the time to think it through and *evaluate* the criticism before taking it to heart, you might discover, regularly, that it's not true for you, or that the "advice" it offers wouldn't work very well for you.

What to do when you're criticized

If someone criticizes you, instead of feeling immediately ashamed or incorrect, see if you can listen to your inner voice. Do you feel like the person is truly trying to help you, or does it seem like they might be trying to make you feel "less-than"? Does the criticism have validity? How often is it true? How often is it not true?

Some criticizers will generalize, meaning that they offer their criticism as if the issue is always or never true, as in "You never pay enough attention to your finances," or "You always overdo your makeup." Unless they're with you 24/7, they don't know how you spend the rest of your time.

Any time a criticizer is generalizing, be sure you consider the comment carefully before just taking it at face value. And remember, it's only their opinion. 90% of the population might feel differently!

Try responding to a criticism with "Thank you. I'll think about that," rather than "Okay" or "I'm sorry." This helps you take time to think about it rather than automatically agreeing to comply. When criticism comes from certain people, we interpret it more as a command or an order, when it is really just disapproval.

You have a choice: you can immediately accept the criticism as true (whether it is or not) and respond accordingly, or consider it first, decide not to take it in, and follow your own choice instead. You may have to tolerate the feelings that come up if you choose to disobey the criticizer (which we'll talk more about in Chapter 2), but you can only create an authentic life by making authentic choices. You can't become authentic by following the paths that others have prescribed for you.

If you decide to do something differently, the criticizer will increase pressure to get you to do what he or she wants—just like a bully does. In fact, repetitive criticism is a form of bullying, even when it happens in families. Just because someone is a parent or caretaker doesn't mean they aren't a bully if they mistreat you.

Start with small things, so you can learn what it feels like to go against the criticizer's wishes. You'll find information about helping yourself feel more comfortable "breaking the family rules" in Chapter 5.

If you find that the tension in the relationship increases when you go against the criticizer's demands, you might consider putting more distance between that person and yourself if you can, or severely limiting the time you spend with them.

Developing the courage to make your own choices and stand your ground will increase your strength, and will help you to separate from the enmeshment (which means that individuals aren't allowed to be separate from the whole) that is so much a part of dysfunctional family dynamics.

The sense of futility: "There's nothing I can do"

Repetitive criticism, whether it happened in the past or is an issue in your current life, can create a sense of futility, causing you to feel as if there's nothing you can do about a situation. But there are always options. When we're criticized over and over, we can lose a sense of our own power—but the power to respond in new ways and to help ourselves heal will always be inside. You do have a choice about what you believe, what you think, and how you behave and respond, whether it feels that way to you right now or not.

If you find yourself falling into a mood where you feel helpless and hopeless, as if nothing will ever change, your psyche is bringing up useful information that can help you move past an issue or obstacle that's standing in your way. We can't begin to free ourselves from a trap of seeing life in a certain way or believing certain things unless we realize that we're in a trap. Only then can we begin to break free.

Experiencing a sense of futility can be a way of denying an immense and terrifying buildup of frustration—a well of distress and disappointment at having needs ignored or belittled time after time after time—and it can affect an adult's relationships, career, and deepest sense of self.

If a small child's needs are not met with at least some regularity, there is a tremendous sense of frustration, of powerlessness to get anything that he or she needs. Over time, as the frustration builds up and is repressed again and again, it becomes too painful to face, and a sense of futility develops. If it isn't acknowledged and allowed expression, the frustration will continue to hide under the surface and grow into a feeling of futility.

Though feeling like it's futile to try to change is unpleasant, it is less threatening and painful than continuous, enormous frustration. Futility is a numbing feeling—it offers the option of not having to feel pain or face and resolve difficult issues.

If you feel hopeless, the first step in getting to a better place is taking a good look at your feelings. Dig under the surface a bit: ask yourself what's causing the hopelessness. Are you frustrated? Are you angry? Sometimes it take a while to get to the root of the feelings, but there is always something underneath a feeling of futility.

Be open to encountering the feelings that come up. Sometimes a sense of futility covers tremendous rage. Denying so much repressed rage requires tremendous energy—energy that could be used to create an authentic and exciting life.

Once you can name what you're feeling, ask yourself what might have caused that feeling. Allow the feeling (sadness or rage, etc.) to arise in your body as you consider the question. Sometimes our bodies have better answers than our minds do— we often hold very important information in our bodies that we don't really want to look at.

It's not always easy to look at our feelings. For one thing, society doesn't encourage it—rather, most of us are encouraged to "suck it up." And emotions aren't allowed in many dysfunctional families—or there may be a message that parents can have emotions, but children can't.

Check your background: was it okay to express feelings in your family? If it wasn't, was there anyone in the family who was allowed to express their emotions (this includes rage, sadness, depression, happiness, enthusiasm, joy, and all and any other emotions)?

If so, how did this person (or people) express their feelings? Did witnessing that expression of emotion give you any beliefs about whether or not it was okay for people to have and vent feelings?

Did you have any other experiences which influenced your thinking about having feelings and exploring or expressing them?

Remember that because we are born with the ability to have feelings, they are a natural and normal part of being human, and you have every right to find healthy ways to express your feelings, even if they're extremely strong ones, like rage or grief.

Here's an example to consider: If a child had a parent who often exhibited rage, it might be more difficult for that child as an adult to admit that he or she is feeling rage, because of a deep-seated fear of expressing anger. The rage of a parent can be terrifying for a young child. But anger is an extremely useful emotion in that it helps us burn away what's false, makes us aware of our needs, and gives us tremendous energy and courage to work on getting our needs met.

Many books have been written on the physical effects of repressed emotions: when they're stuck in our bodies, our energy is stuck, and physical illnesses can affect us later in life.

The more we express our feelings in healthy ways, the healthier our bodies can be.

In Chapter 4, you'll learn a simple system that you can use to let go of difficult feelings, and build your confidence and sense of self.

Beware the drama addiction!

For many families, the idea of reaching out and exploring the magnificence that life has to offer is so frightening that family members close down (sometimes especially as they age), and begin to focus instead on all the "dramas" in the family, adding fuel to each tiny problem and making it dispropor-tionately huge. A glass of spilled milk, muddy shoes on a clean floor, or the way someone chooses to dress for an event or parent their kids are viewed as extremely important subjects, because things like passion for a cause or learning new things or living life to the fullest are too scary.

The Drama Addiction is actually a rather twisted version of a natural way of being—an expression of our passion for life. But in some families, it's not okay to feel good, or to anticipate happiness, or to create with joy, so this natural passion gets twisted into chaos, angst, fear, and highly charged negative criticism.

Recognize that a negative Drama Addiction is just a habitual pattern. It doesn't have to be a way of life, and you can choose to focus on finding excitement in life instead of participating in the drama. Over time and with focus, you can expand your mind and your options rather than succumbing to the small-mindedness of others.

If you find yourself grumping and grousing or criticizing someone else in a drama-addicted way in a family situation, see if you can tune out what's going on around you. Move your focus to the good things in your life and the things (even if they are few) that you like about that person, and let those thoughts inform what you're looking forward to, what you would like to create. And remember that no one is dying, no one is going to the hospital, and the stressful situation can be over as soon as you decide to leave.

If you grew up in a drama-addicted family, you may have a tendency to see most situations as life-or-death, or feel as if there's always an emergency right around the corner, even if things seem peaceful at the moment. Usually this is a result of having had to be hypervigilant as a child—especially if your family situation was chaotic or frightening—and consequently developing a habit of trying to see problems before they even show up.

When situations feel like they're spinning out of control, or it feels like the world is ending, ask yourself, "Is this really that important?" When you feel like your decisions will create life-and-death consequences, sometimes asking yourself, "Will it seem that huge in six months? In five years?" can help you see that maybe it's not as big a problem as you think it is.

Meditation and other practices that reduce stress can be very helpful in overcoming the drama addiction. It's also important to create activities in your life that provide a sense of excitement for you, so you can break away from the negative/false sense of "excitement" that runs alongside criticism through dysfunctional family dynamics, and focus on truly exciting possibilities instead.

Activities like taking dance classes, joining a local community theater, or finding discussion groups that ignite your passion for life are the best antidotes to the drama addiction. What would make life exciting for you? What would allow you to express your passion for life in a positive way? Remember that you don't have to do anything "perfectly."

As adults, we often feel like we should know everything, but in reality, everyone has to learn how to do things from the first day they decide to start. Every dancer and actor once stood in his or her first class not knowing what to do. What's important is that you find something you're passionate about, and focus on that instead of the addiction to family dramas, or unhealthy dramas in other areas of your life.

Sometimes, in order to let go of the drama addiction, we have to just surrender to whatever is happening around us. An addiction to drama can help us feel like we're in control of a situation, even when it's chaotic. Surrendering to what's happening allows more energy to flow into the situation, which can open up blockages and let solutions to problems become more apparent.

Begin to notice where in your life you tend to "catastrophize" (make a catastrophe out of a small event). If you notice yourself getting upset over a small issue, like muddy shoes on the floor, or something that doesn't go the way you expect, stop yourself before you get into a mood about it, and look for a solution.

The drama addiction can be particularly strong in people who've been consistently criticized, because the learned behavior is just to accept the criticism or mishap without evaluating it or looking for a simple solution (i.e., wipe the floor, wipe off the shoes). Life does have problems—as much as we would like it to be perfect, it rarely is. You can let go of the drama addiction by surrendering and looking for solutions rather than catastrophizing.

Chapter 3: Tips for Coping
with Family Bullying

Gossip about other family members, criticism, and out-and-out fighting can quickly ruin a family gathering. To make things worse, memories of family conflicts play through our minds for days or weeks afterwards like a repeating melody from an oldies song.

Family bullies can be even worse than school bullies, and most of the time we think there's nothing we can do but put up with it, get through it, and leave as quickly as possible. But there are ways you can minimize the effects of relating to dysfunctional family members.

Don't take it personally

If you tend to take criticism to heart and immediately accept critical statements as true without evaluating them, as discussed in the last chapter, you are doing yourself a disservice, and you're losing an opportunity to learn more about yourself. "Taking it personally" means to immediately believe a criticism, whether or not the criticizer's statement is actually true.

Some critical people would rather gripe and groan about someone else than try to solve their own problems. So they look for someone else they can complain about, and offer their critical opinions, whether or not those opinions are based in reality. In fact, some people want so badly to feel bigger than other people that they make things up to criticize others about.

When we take bullying and belittling personally, we can start to feel like we're doing a bad job with our lives—even if we're actually doing well—and self-esteem begins to erode one block at a time. And we're losing the opportunity to take an honest look inside and ask ourselves, "Am I really like that? Do I really seem that way to other people?"

As you're going within to evaluate a criticism, you might discover that you're actually *not* who the person is saying you are, that in fact you might have a greater number of good qualities than qualities that deserve criticism.

Sometimes people will bully family members when they feel intimidated by a person's intelligence, capabilities, creativity, talents and skills, and/or accomplishments. People often do this in an effort to "put everyone on the same level," and cut the "brighter" or livelier person down to size.

So allow yourself to be honest with yourself—maybe you're working harder or smarter than someone else, and that's why you've accomplished more, or perhaps you have a natural creative bent which has given you many talents. This is something to be proud of, not to try to hide.

At the very least, find other people with whom it feels safe to be the "biggest" you that you can be, and spend more time with them than the people who cut you down. We're all here to grow and develop, and to keep growing as much toward our potential as we can. Don't let anyone stop you from doing that, at least in one area of your life.

Often, people who criticize or dump anger on family members are actually angry about other things—a rude boss, a coworker who isn't carrying his or her share of the work, or even a spouse or partner with whom they're uncomfortable expressing their anger. They may dump their anger on you because they feel safer doing that than they would if they directly confronted the situation that's actually making them angry.

Here's a good way to cope: let 'em gripe and groan, and pretend you're watching a movie instead of being in the same room with the gripers. Step back and get curious about all the stuff that's going on—see what you can learn—and pretty soon your focus may be on how funny or ludicrous it all is, rather than how painful it feels.

You can also do a reality check with yourself or someone else by asking, "Is this criticism always true?" Perhaps a family member happened to be in a bad mood and felt like griping, so they belittled something you did or said, even if it's not true, or only true once in awhile.

Generalizing: "You always..." and "You never..."

Some family members preface a criticism with "You always..." or "You never..." even when they're talking about a single event or situation. This is one clue that can tell you the other person is probably only looking for an excuse to criticize, because they're blowing up one small issue into a huge all-encompassing life pattern that may not even exist.

Here's another clue to watch out for: Often, criticizers are very good at generalizing with their criticism, so that you can't really put your finger on exactly what they're saying is wrong—you only know that somehow they think you don't measure up (remember, they're often looking to gain a feeling of power, not to help you become a better person).

Generalized comments such as "You should dress better" or "You aren't raising your kids right" are actually meaningless, because they don't provide a specific solution for how to do it "better," and they don't provide any insight into what the actual "problem" might be. People who criticize this way are clearly only putting others down, not offering helpful information.

When critical people denounce others, they don't always necessarily tell the entire truth—and sometimes they don't tell the truth at all. Keep asking yourself, "Is this really true? If it is, is it *always* true, or only occasionally?" And even better, "So, am I okay with having that be true occasionally?"

Most of us take a criticism as an order or commandment, because that's how it's presented. But you always have the option to ignore a criticism, and go on your merry way doing things just the way you were doing them before.

There may be consequences, if the person who's criticizing you has control over some aspect of your life. If so, this is a sign that you need to get some kind of help in taking back control of your life so you're not subject to someone else's whims if they don't have your best interests at heart. If you don't like the idea of therapy or counseling, you might do some of the exercises in the Appendix, or consider an assertiveness training course. The principles you learn can be applied in several areas of your life.

Rather than focusing on your feelings about the criticism, focus on what you think the other person is trying to accomplish by criticizing you. Are they a know-it-all? Could they be feeling less than competent themselves, and need to gain a feeling of being in control by criticizing someone else? This will help you step back so you don't take it so personally.

You can also imagine yourself protected by an energy shield, made of glass or Kryptonite or whatever substance you desire. The shield can allow you to interact with other people, but protect you from the barbs and digs that might come your way, so they bounce off without having any effect.

It's all about control

Some people use criticism, guilt, and shame as a way to control other family members or to goad them into a conflict because they think family fights are more fun to watch than a football game. Some people bully in order to feel powerful. A bully feels weak, powerless, and one-down, so he or she has to put someone else down in order to feel "normal-sized."

Bullying or criticism is not about who you are as much as it's about who they are. Sometimes just pausing for a moment and saying, "Excuse me?" from a strong stance allows the person to actually hear what they've said and realize that you didn't fall for it. This statement can defuse a barrage of condemnation.

Recognize that 90% or more of the criticism that's directed at you may not have anything to do with whether or not you're living your life in the "best" way. You're probably doing what works for you, even though others might do things differently.

Criticism is all about how small the family bully feels inside, and how desperate he or she is to put other people down or control them in order to feel more powerful. It's meant to control you—and if you don't allow it to control your feelings and actions, you're already winning the battle.

If someone has criticized you and brought up a lot of feelings for you, it's extremely important to acknowledge and let go of those feelings as soon as you can, using the system in Chapter 3.

When feelings are denied and build up over time, it's harder to think clearly, which makes it more and more difficult to respond from a place of strength. Expressing feelings freely "opens the channel" to our deepest selves, and allows us to see more clearly what's actually happening in a family situation.

Beware of emotional "dumping"

One of the hallmarks of "Spider Love" is the tendency for some family members to "dump" their negative emotions on children. When they're feeling frustrated or angry and can't acknowledge their feelings or can't confront the source of their anger or frustration, they may get angry at a child without provocation. If you remember times when a parent got angry with you, and you had no idea why, they were probably dumping their anger at someone or something else on you.

Children are often easy targets for this kind of "emotional dumping." They want to please their parents, they may be afraid of abandonment, and it can feel safer for an adult to express anger at a child than it would be to express it to a boss or spouse. Sadly, in dysfunctional families, children are often the repository of most of the anger, fear, shame, and sadness that adults don't want to acknowledge.

Unfortunately, this kind of "dumping" often happens in work situations as well, when supervisors or managers feel a need to "get rid" of their anger or frustration.

Think back in your memory to see if you can find a time that someone got angry at you seemingly for no reason, and realize that their anger may have had nothing at all to do with you. You were most likely doing everything just fine, but simply got caught in the crosshairs of their overwhelming anger.

Some adults also dump pieces of their identity that they're not comfortable with on children—including a sense of lack, feelings of incompetence, or clumsiness or difficulty concentrating. A parent might tell a child, "You're so stupid" simply because they're trying to deny their own feelings of not knowing what to do next. The child might have completely normal or even above-average intelligence, but children believe what their parents tell them, because they have no way to see any other perspective.

Think back to the messages you received about who you were. If focusing on whatever message it was makes you feel a little nauseous (physically, mentally, or emotionally), that message probably included some emotions being dumped on you.

For the stronger, repetitive messages, search your memory for information that disproves the messages. Someone who was called "stupid" as a child might focus on the fact that he or she performs well on the job and generally gets along with most other people, which would disprove the message. Someone who was designated "incapable" in childhood might focus on all the things they can do, and consequently realize that someone else's feelings of incompetence were probably dumped on him or her.

Plan your responses ahead of time

If you know what kinds of comments push your buttons, prepare responses ahead of time that allow you to hold on to your self-esteem. For instance, if someone always comments on your parenting style, you can say, "I parent my kids according to my own values. I'm sorry if you don't like it, but that's what I will continue to do."

Use "I" messages rather than "you" messages, which means saying "I think" or "I feel" rather than "You always" or "You shouldn't." "I" messages keep the focus on what you're trying to communicate, and are less likely to instigate an argument.

Practice your responses several times when you're alone so they become automatic. When you're in the midst of a heated situation, sometimes it's hard to come up with a response that's not habitual, so if you practice beforehand, standing up for yourself will begin to become a positive habit.

You can also try saying, "What are you trying to tell me?" when someone criticizes you. They may be trying to communicate something below the surface of their words, and may only know how to do that through criticism.

Another tactic that often works to defuse criticism is to take a strong stance, look the person right in the eye, pause for a moment, and then say, "Excuse me?" With this phrase, you're letting the person know that you're aware they're putting you down or dumping on you, and you're not going to take it—but the beauty of this phrase is that it's non-confronting: you're not adding fuel to the fire or throwing your anger back at the other person.

You do need to take a strong stance, however, and say the words very clearly. Often, this will stop the criticizer in his tracks as he steps back and hears what he actually said.

Remove yourself from the situation

If you find yourself getting sucked into what the person says, take a break and go somewhere private. You can go in the bathroom and scream silently, shake your hands out, shake your head, let the tension out of your body, and tell yourself you won't get caught up in the drama.

It can take some practice over time to remember to take a break, but by stepping out of the situation over and over, you're reminding yourself of your separateness and your awareness of the dysfunction, and validating your desire to stay out of the traps and become mentally healthier.

If you feel a need to leave the situation altogether, you do have the power to do that. People may get upset or yell or threaten you, but you're not responsible for their feelings—you're not responsible for calming them down, for solving their problems, or for ignoring your own needs in order to make them happy. They'll try to get you under their control again, but the more you pay attention to your own needs and act on them, the more respect you'll develop for yourself.

Set boundaries

Setting boundaries ahead of time can help you feel more in control of a situation. Tell everyone ahead of time that you can only stay for two hours at a family party, or that instead of cooking the holiday ham for the tenth year in a row, this time you'll bring a salad.

You'll need to be prepared for a backlash of "No! You can't change! We liked you better when you let us control you!" But you'll be growing stronger each time you stick to your guns, and each time it'll be easier. Pay attention to your own needs and desires—they're absolutely just as important as anyone else's.

When you've just left a difficult situation, instead of rolling it around and around in your mind, set yourself a mental task of figuring out how to make it easier for yourself next time. What would need to change? How could you respond in a way that helps you feel more centered and grounded? What kinds of boundaries would it help to set up before the next time you see them?

Setting boundaries is a very important life skill that will help you in every area of your life. If you have trouble setting boundaries in your relationships or your work life, you might consider doing some of the exercises in the Appendix, or taking assertiveness training.

When you leave, leave it all behind you

Ruminating over who said what and how awful it all felt for days afterwards is a negative habit that reinforces old emotional patterns. Instead, remind yourself that the situation is over, and allow it to turn into a fading memory rather than constantly pulling it back into the front of your mind to relive over and over again. Keep your focus on how you're growing and what you want to create in your own life, rather than on how others are holding you back.

People who are regularly criticized by others tend to be very critical of themselves as well. Have compassion for yourself, and treat yourself with kindness. Most of us are actually doing a better job at everything than we think we are!—no matter what anyone else believes or says.

Chapter 4: Recovering from
a Dysfunctional Childhood

The only way to truly recover from a dysfunctional childhood and create an authentic life is to face your feelings, acknowledge them, express them freely, and let them go. Feelings are a normal part of being human, and they're meant to be fully expressed.

When we don't face our feelings and learn how to release them, each time a situation comes up that is similar to an experience that caused strong feelings in the past, we become "triggered" by all of the old, unresolved feelings, and we have a tendency to respond in a knee-jerk habitual fashion to the new situation instead of finding innovative, healthier ways to respond.

The more we try to deny feelings instead of expressing them freely, the more they build up in our subconscious minds, and the more power they have over us. What often happens is that unexpressed feelings build up to the point where they absolutely demand expression, which causes situations like road rage or mall shootings, or illness like ulcers, colitis, or heart disease when they're turned inward.

Expressing feelings is easy, once you've made the decision to honor yourself enough to let go of the emotions that have been dragging you down—whether you feel anger, shame, sadness, grief, frustration, or a sense of hopelessness. Sometimes it's a little difficult to begin, especially if you've been in the habit of shoving your feelings down for years or decades.

The following section will help you begin.

Become a witness for your emotional self

Imagine that a part of you will act as a "witness" to your feelings as you go through this process—as if you're being a friend to yourself while you express your feelings. You could think of the "witness" as your soul, or a higher power, or the memory of a grandmother or other person who helped you feel safe and loved.

Part of you can stand outside of what you're thinking and feeling, as if you're watching what goes on inside of you from another perspective, in the same way that sometimes we "watch" ourselves in social situations.

See if you can feel the love that flows to you from this part of you. In our society, we're taught that it's okay to love others, but not ourselves. However, loving yourself is all-important in the process of creating a life that works for you, a life that is truly your own.

Most people judge themselves harshly, but have compassion and forgiveness for the faults in others. Have compassion for yourself as well—you're doing the best you can with your life given your circumstances.

This "witness" part of you will help you feel in control of the process, so you're not afraid that you'll "go over the edge" or go crazy as you let go of the feelings. You can say comforting things to yourself while you let go of the feelings, like "I'm so sorry that happened," or "I totally understand what you're feeling."

The witness aspect of you is different from the part of you that thinks and feels and remembers. Some people might call it your spirit, and some people might think of it as an "inner parent" who comforts the "inner child" in the process. This is the aspect of you that needs to have compassion for yourself as you explore your emotions.

The four steps to recovery

There are four steps in the process of moving beyond old feelings:

1. Figure out and acknowledge what you're feeling—is it shame? Sadness? Despair? Anger? You may have to dig a bit inside in order to uncover what emotions are troubling you the most. Keep asking yourself, "What's really going on? What am I feeling?" Think about where you feel the feeling—is it in your stomach? Is there a tightness in your throat or neck? Do your shoulders want to hunch?

Alice Miller, a psychologist who's written numerous excellent books on recovering from a difficult childhood, wrote a book called The Body Never Lies. This is absolutely true: if you listen to your body, it will tell you everything you need to know about how you're feeling and what really happened in a situation. Trust your body and your instincts to tell you the truth.

2. Once you've figured out what you're feeling, find a private place, and let yourself express that feeling: cry, punch sofa pillows, shake your fists, throw rocks into a pond—whatever helps. With part of your mind acting as your "witness" standing off to the side, let your body do whatever it wants to do.

You can also journal about what's going on, but the feelings will move out faster if they're *physically* expressed, because emotions are stored in the musculature of the body when they can't be expressed and can eventually turn into physical illness (i.e., ulcers, heart disease, high blood pressure, etc.).

The more you can release your pent-up feelings, the more of the past you'll clear away. Go to a sad movie and cry buckets, or whack a bed with a plastic bat—whatever works for you. Releasing emotions releases energy, which you can then use to create a more authentic life.

3. Tell yourself you can let go of the feelings, and allow them to drift out of your body and mind. Sometimes we have a tendency to hold on to feelings, because at some point it was safer to hold on than to express them, so we had to keep pushing them down inside. You don't have to keep holding them in any more.

Call up the witness part of you to comfort yourself as you let the emotions go, and remind yourself that what you're feeling is not who you are, it's only a feeling that will pass.

If it seems like you can't let go of the feeling, ask yourself, "Why? What do I need to look at? What is holding me back from letting go?" A past event or experience will often surface if you ask with a sense of curiosity and let yourself be open to any answer that comes. You may need to go back to Step 2 if this is the case.

Repeating the questions over the course of several days gives your subconscious mind time to bring the issue to the surface, and you may find that it's easier to let go of it piece by piece instead of all in one fell swoop.

When someone hurts us, it's human nature to hold on to the hurt, because we think that somehow, if we can figure it out, it won't be as painful. But you hurt yourself all over again when you hold on to a bad feeling—thinking about past experiences over and over can drag you down and make you miserable over time. It's much better to let them go, just let their energy drift away. Once you do, you can see everything a little more clearly, and be a little more in touch with your authentic self.

4. After you've let go of some feelings, call a supportive friend to talk about something else, go to a movie, or join a group that's going to a fun place—help yourself remember that life can be good. Anything you enjoy doing is fine. This step helps you remember that there are good things in life, and helps you refocus on what you enjoy as the darker emotions drift away.

Take as much time as you need for this process. Feelings that have been denied for years or decades need space to express themselves. And any time you notice tension in your body, or your mind begins to race, ask yourself if you need to let go of some feelings.

If you've experienced a deep betrayal of your innermost self at some time in your life, your processing time may be longer than someone who hasn't had many traumatic experiences. For some people, recovery can take months or years—but this makes sense when you consider that the frustrations, the hurts, the anger probably built up over a period of many years.

Be sure to be compassionate with yourself as you go through the process, and if you find yourself in emotional water that seems deeper than you can still navigate, be sure to seek help and support.

It takes tremendous courage to look at how the past has affected us, and tremendous courage to work through the pain. Get help if you feel yourself floundering.

More ways to express feelings

Art is an excellent venue for expressing feelings. Get some paints and paper, and let the feelings run out of you onto the paper. Use dark colors if the feelings are sad, reds and yellows if you're angry.

Try finger-painting, which allows the body full expression of feelings—let yourself go, and imagine your difficult feelings moving out of you and becoming a picture on the paper.

It doesn't matter whether you're an artist or not—what's important is getting the feelings out. You can toss the paintings as soon as you're done if you want to.

Dancing or weightlifting or other forms of exercise can also be a great outlet for feelings. Turn on your favorite music and let your body just move and flow, following the emotions that the music creates in you.

Punching a punching bag is a great way to express anger, and shaking your head and hands and body is very helpful in letting go of fear. Punching a pillow is another great outlet, and works even better when you allow yourself to express your feelings vocally—i.e., "You made me *so mad* when you did that! I just wanted to get back at you!"

One of the biggest issues in our society is stress and anxiety—and living in an anxious, stressed condition can cause great damage to the body. Many people spend a huge amount of energy trying to deny or repress their fear. But as with any other emotion, the more you stuff the fear down, the bigger the pile grows, until it becomes a major, constant experience of anxiety.

It may seem odd that the best way to relieve anxiety is to express the fear whenever it comes up, but it's true—the more you give attention to allowing and letting go of the fear, the less it will bother you over time.

One of the best ways to let go of fear and stress is to move your body—whether it's exercise like walking, or simply heading to the nearest restroom to shake the tension out of your body. If you watch young children who've been very scared, once the scary experience is past, they're usually shaking and trembling or moving their arms and legs.

If your feelings seem totally overwhelming and more than you can handle, you might consider seeing a counselor or therapist for a period of time, or finding a support group in your area or online. This is one of the ways we can learn tools for taking better care of ourselves and recovering from a difficult history.

It's always prudent to seek help if your emotions seem overpowering, or if you find that they prevent you from functioning in life. Seeking help does not mean a person is weak, it is simply an opportunity to learn how to take better care of the self, and to receive emotional support through a tough time. But you can do the work on your own if it's easier for you.

If you continue this process over a period of time, eventually the old feelings will become a memory, rather than a shadow that lives with you day in and day out, and you'll be living more from your authentic self than from your past experiences.

When you pay attention to the relationship between how you experience life now and what life was like as you grew up, you'll begin to see correlations between what you learned early on and what you're experiencing in life now.

The psyche tends to "repeat" old patterns in order to get our attention—and the more attention you pay to investigating and releasing old beliefs and recovering from your old patterns, the faster recovery will happen.

By developing the "witness" aspect of your inner self, you can simultaneously feel what's happening in the moment, and also get a larger view of what's really going on deep within the psyche. This allows for a process of "sorting through" the tangled web of beliefs, behaviors, and self-images created in childhood in order to get along within a dysfunctional family.

It's important to write down the insights that filter up from your subconscious mind. The process of recovering from trauma, uncovering your authentic self, and learning new ways of relating to the world is enhanced by seeing the feelings and new perceptions that come to you in front of you on paper.

Otherwise, if you're relying on your memory to hold on to your new understanding, it's pretty likely that your insights will slip back into your subconscious mind under the pressure of your old patterns of thinking, believing, and behaving.

As you begin to see yourself, your family, and the old, outmoded behavior patterns that run your life with more clarity, you're taking steps to live more deeply from your authentic self. The path will move forward quickly at times, and at other times you may feel stuck in the past. It's a two-steps forward, one-step back process as you retrain yourself to think and behave in more positive ways. Stick with it, and you'll discover that your life is getting better and better!

Chapter 5: Understanding the "Rules" in Your Family

The first step in learning to connect with your authentic self if to get in touch with your natural thinking process. You were born with an incredible ability to learn and grow, to develop into a uniquely gifted human being, to fulfill your potential as a distinct and creative individual. But the beliefs and behavior patterns you learned throughout your childhood years can be holding you back from being the best that you can be, and from creating a fulfilling life for yourself.

You can encourage your natural intelligence by doing some thinking about your family's rules, and how they affected you as a child. Ask yourself the following questions as you remember what it was like for you back then.

- Did you feel generally supported by the rules, by your family's ways of doing things? Or did you feel restricted by them?
- Were there unspoken rules that you knew you had to follow, as well as rules that were more clearly laid out?
- Were the reasons for the rules and specific ways of doing things explained to you, or were you expected to follow what was set out for you without understanding why?

If your answer to the last question is yes, you may be especially susceptible to criticism, because you were never taught how to evaluate the information coming in—you were simply expected to comply.

Parents are sometimes distracted or too busy with the details of life to explain the reasoning behind rules in a way that children can understand. What can happen if the rules are not explained to a child is that he may begin to believe that the rest of the world functions in exactly the same way that his family does. He'll accept those rules as laws of the world—as "just the way it is."

Children have no frame of reference with which to understand that those rules are simply *choices* that his parents have made, and that other families and communities will have different styles of relating and behaving. His focus becomes narrow, he becomes less flexible, and may have trouble as an adult operating outside of the rules set for him by his parents.

You can gain more flexibility, depth, and breadth in your thinking by reevaluating the rules you were taught as a child. You may still be living your life based on some outmoded principles, and your perspective as an adult is much broader than it was when you were small, so you're better able to judge now whether or not a particular belief or pattern of behavior still works for you.

As you examine these rules, you'll begin to see which ones are holding you back, and which may still be useful to you as an adult. The more specific you are in your examination of the past, the easier it will be for you to discover the roots of your conditioned beliefs, and get in touch with your authentic self.

Dedicate a page in your journal to the following exercise. Writing your answers down will clarify your thoughts.

Uncovering the family rules

- What were the specific rules in your family? Take a moment to name some of them for yourself.
- How did you feel about each rule?
- Are those feelings similar to feelings your experience now surrounding current problems in your life?
- Do you feel as if you're still required to follow those old rules? If so, why?
- Can you think of different ways the rules might be worded or expressed so that they could serve you better in your adult life? Or are some of the rules no longer even valid for you as an adult?

Obviously, some of the rules you were taught as a child can be helpful in your adult life: "Look both ways before you cross the street" can keep you safe; "Don't talk with your mouth full" can assure that you'll continue to be invited to social occasions. But admonitions such as "Don't talk back!" or "Don't touch anything!", when carried into adult life, an make it very difficult to express yourself and to move forward in creating a rewarding life.

In particular, "Don't talk back!" can prevent you from defending yourself against family bullies, potentially difficult situations, and even workplace bullying. If this was one of the rules in your family, reevaluating whether or not it's useful for you (and in what situations) can help you learn to communicate more clearly and openly with others, protect yourself, and express your emotions more freely and appropriately.

"Don't talk back!" causes children to repress feelings and self-expression, which can result in frustration and withdrawal. If you feel held back from expressing yourself fully, and from exploring and experiencing life in all its depth and diversity, you may still be following old family rules that no longer work for you.

As an adult, you have enough knowledge and life experience to take good care of yourself, and you don't need to blindly follow childhood rules any longer in order to keep yourself safe. You have the freedom to make new rules for yourself, and the right to live and respond in whatever way you choose.

Unspoken rules

Unspoken rules in families are rules that are not necessarily clearly laid out, but are still part of the family's code of behavior. Rules such as "Don't get in Mom's way when she's cooking" or "Leave Dad alone when he's reading the paper" are communicated and enforced by a family member's behavior (facial expressions and body language) and/or by response when the rule is being violated.

For instance, Mom might sigh in exasperation, ignore questions, or bang pots and pans. Dad might rustle his paper or answer with noncommittal sounds. When a child carries unspoken rules into adulthood, he or she may try to determine what others are thinking based on their behavior rather than their words, and because behavior can be based on a variety of motivations, this can cause blocks in communication.

Unspoken rules can go even deeper: if a child is rarely touched with affection and gentleness, she'll probably grow up feeling unworthy of affection, and may have difficulty as an adult responding to her own or others' feelings with kindness and concern. Because those qualities were never demonstrated, they're not part of her repertoire.

Or if a child is not treated with respect, and allowed to express ideas and emotions, he'll grow up feeling as if he doesn't really matter, except in terms of how well he can follow the rules and "produce" what's expected.

Some families are tremendously structured around unspoken rules. Everyone in the family knows the "invisible" rules, and the behavior of all family members is based on them. But taking those unspoken rules into adulthood can create misunderstandings and misinterpretations when communicating with anyone who is not part of the family.

Unspoken rules can be more difficult to pinpoint than rules which are clearly laid out, because they often affect a child on several different levels at one. By the same token, once you examine them, they can also yield a richer connection with your authentic self, because they may be holding you back in a number of different ways. For the following exercise, it's helpful to verbalize the unspoken rules for yourself, and then examine your responses—physically, mentally, and emotionally.

- What were the unspoken rules in your family? List as many as you can think of in your journal, verbalizing them as you write.
- Did any members of your family use behavior and action, rather than words, to let you know what was and what wasn't allowed?
- What did you think they were trying to communicate?
- How did the other person's behavior make you feel?
- Did you feel you had a choice as to how to respond? If so, what choice did you make? If not, how did you feel about not having a choice?
- Were there consequences for breaking the rules? If so, what were they?

These questions may bring up some very deep and uncomfortable feelings. This is absolutely normal—deep-seated and long-repressed feelings gain power the longer they are avoided and denied, sometimes gathering a huge well of sorrow and anger.

If these questions bring up strong feelings for you, please review the sections on expressing feelings in Chapter 4, and allow yourself to take as much time as you need to express your emotions, until the feelings subside. Though it can be very uncomfortable, letting yourself release pent-up feelings will help you feel better in the long run, and contributes to your mental and physical health.

Remember that the situation was different for you when you were a child, and that as an adult you can now make your own choices about expressing your feelings and responding to the behavior of others.

Shaming

Sometimes adults will shame children in order to get them to follow the rules. "You know better!" or "What do you think you're doing?" are statements designed to shame a child. If the adults in your family shamed you, you might feel a strong inner resistance to moving beyond the rules in your family and creating new rules (boundaries) that work better for you, because you're worried about getting shamed again. This is where compassion for yourself and being nonjudgmental about what is true for you is extremely important.

Family rules in dysfunctional families are usually set up to benefit only one or two of the family members, not everyone. Shame is used to control those family members who are not benefitting from the rules. John Bradshaw, a well-known family therapist, wrote a wonderful book on healing shame, *Healing the Shame that Binds You.* I highly recommend it.

People criticize others for many reasons—to gain control, to feel bigger, to look more important—and also to "dump" their own shame on others. This is usually a generational family pattern, passed down from parents to children. The criticizer is feeling bad and ashamed about something, and rather than taking an honest look inside and changing what is bothering them, they dump their shame on someone else by criticizing so that they feel better, and the shame seems to go away for awhile. Most people aren't even aware that they're doing this.

Some children are sensitive enough that they can actually feel the dark energy of the shame "dumping" on them, but they don't have the experience or the words to know what's going on. They only know how bad it feels.

If you think this might be happening to you as an adult, the next time someone criticizes you—just to see what happens— pretend you have invisible mirrors all around you, so that whatever is coming at you is reflected back. Notice if you feel any differently than you usually do. Notice how the other person responds.

So much energy is passed between people that we can't see or hear. But sometimes we can feel it. If you can feel someone's love coming toward you, then you're sensitive enough to pick up someone's shame coming at you, too.

If you're a sensitive person, there are several books in the Recommended Reading section that can help you handle your sensitivity. I also recommend *Subtle Energy* by William Collinge, Ph.D., which provides some information on the invisible energy exchange between people.

How to change or disobey a family rule

A good way to take the first step toward creating new rules that work for you is to choose one rule from childhood that no longer applies to you as an adult, and deliberately and consciously change it. For example, many children are taught to do whatever they're told to do. Even if they don't want to do something, they learned that they had to say "Yes." As adults, this can translate into feeling like we have to say "Yes" whenever we're asked to do something, only to find later that we have no desire to participate.

One way to change this rule for yourself is to decide that the next time someone asks you to do something, you'll tell them that you have to check your schedule, and that you'll get back to them. This gives you time to decide whether you really want to participate or not. If you don't, you can just tell the person, "Thank you, but not this time." This takes some practice for those of us who are used to saying yes to everything! The key is to give yourself some space to think about it rather than responding with a knee-jerk "Okay."

If this rule was very strongly enforced when you were small, you may need to spend some time when you're alone just getting used to saying "No." Say it in every tone of voice, say it loudly, say it softly, shake your head, turn your body away. Practicing saying "No" will probably generate strong feelings for you. That's okay—you're learning how to express and manage your feelings. And it is absolutely your right to say no to anything you want to, no matter what other people think.

Whenever you work on changing a rule from your past, it's important to remind yourself that you are completely safe now, that as an adult you have power and understanding that you did not have as a child, and that you have the perfect right to choose what you want to do or not do, and who to spend your time with. The "inner child" aspect of you that was hurt and shamed so many years ago is still deep within you, and the more you can reassure that part of you that you're taking care of yourself, the safer you'll feel over time.

Think about what kind of "antidote" you might apply as you change an old rule. For instance, if the rule was "Don't touch anything," you can spend an afternoon walking around your home and touching everything that appeals to you. Or if it was "Always clean your plate before you have dessert," see what happens when you choose to eat your dessert halfway through your meal. Don't want the rest of the vegetables? No problem! You're making your own choices now.

Notice what kinds of feelings come up for you as you allow yourself to break some of the rules from your past—if you find yourself feeling afraid, sad, or angry, release the feelings in whatever way seems appropriate, and remind yourself again that as an adult, you can keep yourself safe. This is difficult work, and the more you can support yourself through the process, the faster it will go and the faster you will grow.

Deciding to change or break one of the rules of your childhood can make you feel like you're being disobedient. This is a natural feeling—but you may need to sit with this emotion and allow yourself to "disobey" in order to facilitate change in your life. As an adult, you won't be punished for disobeying, because you're in charge of your own life now.

Ponder some of the spoken or unspoken rules from your childhood, and choose one that you want to disobey. It could be something like "Don't talk to strangers," "Don't be too good," or "Always do what your parents tell you to do." The next time you have an impulse to say or do something that goes against the rule, notice what happens as you begin to feel the feeling or think the thought.

Does some part of you want to shut down, or try to minimize the impulse so that you behave or respond in a particular way in order to follow the rule?

- Can you identify that part of you?
- If it's a voice in your head, whose voice is it?
- If it's a physical feeling, where does it originate in your body?

Try letting yourself follow the impulse to ignore the rule, and notice again what happens.

- Does the voice in your head become louder or more insistent?
- Does it tell you that you're wrong, or make you feel guilty?
- Does the physical feeling get stronger?
- What would you say if you chose to talk back to the voice, or to reassure the part of your body that wants to follow the rule in order to keep you safe?

You may need to practice moving beyond the rule several times before you begin to feel comfortable with the new perspective. Since you've lived most of your life based on believing the rule was true, it will take some time for you to get comfortable with new styles of behaving and responding. But you'll discover a new sense of freedom when you realize on a deep level that you don't have to live by the old rules anymore.

You can use questions like those above to not only move beyond the old rules, but also to discover the differences between the responses you learned from others and the expression of your authentic self. Try making up your own questions, and let your natural intelligence guide you in finding more ways to investigate your childhood and express your authentic self.

Here's the process in a nutshell: Choose one rule from your childhood, and first examine how it made you feel when you were young. Then think of a situation in your current life that causes those feelings to come up for you again, or one in which the old rule still holds sway.

Now put your natural thinking process to work, and come up with a few options as to how you could bend the rule, or reword / redesign it to make it work for you, or how you could help yourself feel more comfortable discarding it if it's no longer relevant.

If this process doesn't work for you, try sitting down in a private place the next time you feel confused, frustrated, or angry, and asking, "What's going on here? What am I feeling? Why am I feeling this way?"

We tend to treat ourselves the way we were treated as children—denying ourselves the attention we need, pushing feelings out of awareness, and insisting that we put the rules in front of our own well-being.

If you keep asking yourself these kinds of questions, and giving yourself the time and attention you need to explore the issues, eventually the answers will start to come, and the insights and awareness you'll discover inside of yourself will strengthen and encourage your trust in yourself and your ability to make positive changes.

The more you can exercise your thinking process in this way, the easier it will become to pinpoint the similarities between then and now, to ferret out the reasons for current issues, and to gain clarity on the distinction between the beliefs and behavior patterns you learned as a child and the authentic self you've always had inside.

Change can be frightening, particularly to those who grew up with a rigid set of rules and were taught that their natural impulses were unacceptable. As you learn to be patient with yourself, have compassion for yourself, and give yourself as much attention as you can, you'll find that the work becomes part of the fabric of your life—leading you in new directions, offering new possibilities, and helping you to love and express yourself and create the life you want.

Chapter 6: Reclaiming Your Authentic Self

In most dysfunctional families, children are brought up with a certain set of values—firm ideas about how to behave and what to believe, and a set of rules for what is "right" and "wrong" in life. Since they may not be allowed to develop in a way that helps them to create a strong sense of self, they may sometimes "adopt" aspects of a caretaker's personality in the attempt to create a self-identity.

In this chapter, you'll learn how you can separate aspects of your true self from qualities you may have taken on, adopted, or mimicked from others, and begin to discover and create an authentic self. This is a process that Carl Jung called "individuation."

Trapped in the mirror

Sometimes, our habitual feelings, actions, and responses are nothing more than an imitation of someone who needed us to be like them. We may have learned early on to "mirror" someone else, to be like them, in order to be safe or to be loved.

For example, if a parent struggles with depression, a child may grow up with a sense of "commiserating" in that person's habitual gloom. It's hard to be happy when someone else is feeling down—sometimes a child may imitate a parent's mood as a way of identifying with them or making them feel better. Misery does love company.

As an adult, that child may believe that being depressed is just part of who he or she is, when in fact it could have just been a coping mechanism learned in order to get along, because it was hard to share excitement about something good when someone else was despondent. When we're in frequent contact with someone who's depressed and miserable (or angry, or frustrated), it's difficult not to pick up their mood, even if it's not truly a part of who we are.

Children may adopt all kinds of character qualities and aspects of their parents' personalities when they're not allowed to develop in their own authentic way. They mimic responses to life situations (one of the ways the "drama addiction" becomes a habit), handling situations in ways that are similar to the way their parents responded.

Over time, these qualities and habits of response become part of a child's identity, worn like a cloak—because if the child wasn't allowed to develop an identity based on the true self, he or she will adopt the characteristics of a role model in order to have some semblance of self-image and experience a sense of identity. And when children become adults, if they haven't examined the way they relate to life, they often continue to use those same responses even though those responses create obstacles to living life fully.

Journaling is a good way to sort out which aspects of your personality you might have adopted from your parents. You can make a list of the attributes your parents have or had, and go through the list to see which ones you exhibit in your own life. Ask yourself, "Is this really me? Or is it a way of being that I adopted in order to get along?"

Attributes that you might have taken on in order to get along include emotional states, ways of seeing the world (i.e., "everyone is against me" or "nobody's honest anymore"), beliefs about human nature ("we're all sinners" or "we have to be perfect"), beliefs about money ("there's never enough" or "rich/poor people are always _____"), habitual body postures, gestures, and facial expressions, and even personal tastes in food, clothing, environment, and social activities.

Make a separate list of attributes that you feel are really your own—things that you really like, enjoy, or believe in—that you know you didn't take on from your parents, and compare the two. How do the qualities you know are singularly "yours" differ in feeling from the qualities you might have assumed from someone else? You might even make a list for each parent or caretaker to gain more clarity.

When you feel like you're finished with the list, put it away so that your subconscious mind can work on the issue, and take it out again a week later to review. Check in with your body to see whether each of the qualities on both lists still resonate as part of who you are, or whether you've discovered some new insights with the passage of time.

In dysfunctional families, the "we" of a family is usually very strong, whereas individual identities are submerged. The way to begin recovering and discovering your authentic self is to sort out which parts of the self you've known up to now (your identity) are really authentic, and which were simply part of the "we" of your family, which you adopted in order to get along. This is an ongoing process, which will help you develop your own individual identity to depths that you weren't able to reach as a child.

You might also try making a list of your parents' values and beliefs, and follow the above procedure, making a list of your own values and beliefs to compare. If your parents valued a spotless house, do you truly value the same thing, or do you have a different value? Maybe you'd rather meet your friends and have fun, and clean once a month instead of once a week. That's perfectly fine—everyone has different values.

Perhaps your parents valued money and security above everything else, but as a different person, you have an absolute right to decide that you value something else more, if you feel differently than they did.

Remember to have compassion for yourself as you go through the process. If you find this kind of exercise helpful, there are more exercises in the Appendix which can help you get clear on some of the ways in which you learned to think and believe in ways that don't work for you.

Focus on what you enjoy

One of the best ways to encourage the authentic aspects of yourself to emerge is to focus on what you love doing. Some of us were taught that enjoyment and pleasure are wrong, so we fear taking the time to do what we love because we don't want to feel guilty. At the same time, when we get to the end of our lives, most of us will probably wish we spent more time enjoying ourselves. The choice is always up to you as to which way to go.

Many people are brought up to believe that their impulses and intuitions are wrong or misguided, but often, the reason parents stifle their children's impulses toward pleasure or enjoyment is because they feel they need to control the children—or because they have impulses of their own that they're not comfortable with, and find it hard to watch another allowing full expression of their joy and freedom.

Parenting is a very difficult job, and many parents come to it with their own dysfunctional patterns in place. If they haven't done much work to increase their own clarity, they'll respond to their children pretty much the same way their own parents responded to them. This is why dysfunctional family patterns are often handed down from generation to generation.

If your family life was difficult and distressing, with few happy moments, it will feel unfamiliar and strange to you to focus on what you enjoy. You might feel guilty, or wrong, or even "bad" for focusing on what you like and on the process of growing your authentic self. But the habit of avoiding good feelings and turning away from developing your authentic self and your self-esteem is simply another dysfunctional pattern learned in the family, passed down through the generations.

By focusing on what you enjoy, you are actually giving life to the divinely inspired gifts that you were given in this lifetime. Everyone has a unique gift to offer the world, and we are meant to offer our gifts in joy and happiness.

If you grew up with a lot of "shoulds," recognize that those "shoulds" may be holding you back from reaching your highest potential, from bringing forth what is most magnificent within you.

Dysfunctional families often have so many "shoulds" that there's no room for a child to develop his or her own strengths and gifts. The next time you find yourself feeling like you "should" do a particular thing, stop first and ask yourself, "Why should I do this?"

If the answer is that it's something you feel intuitively guided to do, then it's probably right for you. But if your answer is, "Because it's how we always did things in my family," you might want to think twice about following that directive.

Sometimes, in order to be authentic, we actually have to actively disobey the family rules. This can be extremely difficult for people who were shamed or abused for disobeying in childhood. But it's a necessary aspect of individuation.

Many people go through this disobedient stage as teenagers, stretching all the envelopes and breaking rules in order to find out who they really are and gain a sense of internal strength.

If your teenage years were not rebellious, you may have never learned that it's necessary to disobey in order to move forward in your own authentic way. Take small steps—if one of the rules was to turn the water off while brushing your teeth, or never leave clothing lying around, for example, try disobeying one small rule, and see what happens.

Have compassion for yourself here as well. We all have different amounts of fear and anxiety around the rules in our families of origin—but sometimes overcoming that fear and breaking the rules is truly the best way to discover who we really are and what kind of potential we might have for greatness.

Follow your intuition

One of the best ways to unearth your authentic self is by learning to probe your intuition or gut instincts, and respond accordingly. Children in dysfunctional families often have superbly tuned intuition—it helps keep them safe in a chaotic environment—but are usually taught to ignore their own instincts.

Your intuition is actually the best guide to the right life for you. The next time you're in the process of making a decision, get quiet and ask for feedback from within yourself. Ask your intuition for input. You don't have to follow it impulsively all the time, but instinct can offer a much deeper level of knowledge than logic, and its knowledge is based on the totality of who you are, not just on logic or the dictates of family or society.

Don't be surprised if your instincts lead you in wildly divergent directions from the life and self you knew as a child. When parents insist that their children "follow in their footsteps," the amazing uniqueness of each child is cut off, though it remains subconsciously planted in the psyche. Following your intuition reconnects you with the self you were meant to be, and can guide you into a life that works much better for you as an individual.

It may take some time to get reacquainted with your intuition and learn to trust it, especially if your family was extremely dysfunctional. Start with small steps: when you're running errands, tune in to your gut instinct and ask which to do first, or when you're going out to socialize, ask yourself what you would truly enjoy rather than just doing the usual or the expected. When you have a day off, think about what you'd like to do with the time, instead of just focusing on tasks to be done.

If you're looking for a job, or interested in a relationship, try stepping back, listening to your intuition, and letting the Universe bring you opportunities and possibilities, rather than rushing right out to try to resolve the situation. Intuition can be a great friend, and an inspiration for you to co-create with the Universe the life you really want to live.

Support and encourage yourself

One of the best habits you can develop to raise your self-esteem is the practice of encouraging and supporting yourself. In functional families, children are encouraged by parents, and as they become adults, they internalize those supportive voices so that the positive messages are with them for their entire lives. In the same way, those of us who grew up in dysfunctional families internalized the negative, critical voices, which haunt us until we decide we're not going to listen to them any more.

Our society teaches us to look outside of ourselves for support and recognition, and to base our self-image on whether or not we're getting recognition and positive responses from others. This is part of why constant criticism can be so damaging, because many children learn early on to refer to other people before deciding whether something is right for him or her. We never learned to take the time to pat ourselves on the back, or even notice what a good job we've done.

Remember the old adage, "You can't please all the people all the time?" When you base your self-image and self-esteem on the opinions of others, your opinion of yourself will go up and down, and if you're still coping with dysfunctional family members who denigrate or belittle you, your self-esteem will fall every time you take one of the negative comments personally.

It may feel a little odd at first to tell yourself, "That was a job well done" or "I can do this if I try," but over time it'll get easier. Research suggests that we have about 60,000 thoughts a day, and if the majority of those are negative or self-put-downs, we'll feel worse and worse as the day goes on. If you can start tipping the balance so that more and more of your thoughts are self-encouraging, you'll start feeling better and better the more you develop this habit.

Psychologists call this "self-talk"—literally, "the way we talk to ourselves." Talk to yourself as you would to a growing child whose gifts you want to encourage. After so many years of belittling and mistreatment in a dysfunctional family, you might find yourself drinking up the encouragement like nectar from heaven.

In fact, the pictures you show yourself in your mind can be even more powerful in their influence of your thoughts, beliefs, feelings, and behaviors. When you're doing simple tasks like washing dishes or cleaning, try to notice what kinds of pictures go through your mind—especially the pictures that are related to problematic issues in your life. With some attention and practice, you can change the pictures in your mind to images that are much more conducive to creating the life you want to live.

And finally...

Healing from a difficult childhood is not a quick-fix proposition. It takes time to develop new habits, and energy to keep yourself from falling into old ruts of feeling like you have no options but to keep going along in the same old way. Try not to get discouraged; instead, keep focusing on the fact that you're healing from trauma, and allow yourself to explore all the options available to you.

There are always options in life—and you may not have been aware of that up until now, because there often are not a lot of options in a dysfunctional family. Be open to other options and new possibilities as much as you can, and know that you can trust yourself to handle whatever comes up.

Most people in the world will not treat you the same way your dysfunctional family did. It takes a while to begin to see that the world is different than the family atmosphere. The more time you can spend thinking about what you want, noticing what situations in the present remind you of the past and releasing the related emotions, and encouraging yourself in what you most want to do, the more quickly you can heal from the past.

With every strand of the dysfunctional family tapestry you unravel, you'll become more clear on the ways in which you learned to interact dysfunctionally with the world and other people, and as you allow yourself to let the old patterns go and follow your intuition to create new ways of responding to the world, your life will get better and better.

We can only become enlightened by acknowledging and releasing what weighs us down: the shadow aspect of the psyche that carries the burden of the past.

A final note: Some family members are so dysfunctional that the only way to heal from the situation is to break off contact completely, or set severe limits on the amount of time you spend with that person. Though you may feel a little guilty—especially if the family member is very needy, or very hooked into the "Spider Love" approach to loving you—breaking off contact for a period of time, or setting strict limits on how much time you'll spend with them, may be just what you need in order to grow and discover who you are.

If the idea of not having to cope with a particular family member gives you a sense of profound relief, I suggest that you find a counselor or other person who can support you through the process of separation from that person or people.

Remember that you can't fix other people's problems. Nothing you do will remove the misery they feel, if they don't want to let go of it. Being a scapegoat or whipping post for someone else's anger, frustration, grief, or misery is really only enabling them to stay in the same old patterns. There's absolutely nothing wrong with removing yourself from a difficult situation and getting on with your life.

I wish you peace and healing.

Appendix: Exercises

Here are some exercises which can help you blast away some of the illusions you grew up with and reclaim your authentic self:

1. Pretend you're a person of the opposite sex, and review your early life from that perspective with an eye toward the ways in which your childhood might still be affecting the way you live now. Imagine you know nothing about your life except for what could be seen from the outside.

This exercise helps you to truly step outside of your own identity and see the scope of your life from a totally new perspective, and encourages you to embrace the anima/animus (archetypal male/female) aspects of your psyche, which expands and balances your sense of self.

2. Sit down with pen and paper (or computer keyboard) and list three difficult situations that seem to keep recurring in your life, no matter how hard you try to do them differently each time. Do those situations remind you of anything (or anyone) from childhood? Uncovering an unconscious constellation of emotions from the past can help you free yourself from persistent difficulties.

Recurring situations usually mean that your psyche is trying to call something to your attention in order to heal the past experience. If you can pinpoint the past situation that seems to keep showing up in recurring experiences in the present, write about it in your journal, and spend some time expressing the feelings that come up. Over time, similar situations will hold less of a charge for you and occur less frequently.

3. List five qualities of your identity that you've always wanted to change, and take some time to consider whether you feel they're actually part of your authentic self—or whether you "adopted" those qualities in order to get along, or because someone needed you to be like them.

Who do those qualities remind you of? If they don't feel authentic to you, think about qualities you could "replace" them with—in this way you can actually create aspects of your identity and become more as you would like to be.

Here's an example: if someone in your family was always steeped in misery and depression, ask yourself if you might have mirrored those qualities in order to get along with them or help them feel better (or to avoid the guilt of being in a good place when someone else was feeling bad). Do those qualities feel like part of who you really are?

If not, imagine yourself just letting go of misery, letting it float out of your consciousness, and be willing to see who you are underneath. If you have trouble letting go of the feeling, do something that you enjoy, or something that makes you feel good, and narrow your focus to that activity and the good feelings it generates.

Bring only a small part of your mind to the old feeling of misery (don't get caught up in it, and don't allow it to take over your mood), and see if it's easier to let go of when you're in the midst of enjoying yourself.

Who would you be without that old feeling of misery? How would you feel? Over the next few days, focus on your new feeling of identity so it expands into more areas of your life.

4. The next time your reaction to a situation seems out of proportion to what happened, find some privacy as soon after the experience as you can, and try to figure out whether the situation felt familiar in any way. When our reactions are out of proportion, it usually means an old situation or constellation of emotions has been triggered.

Emotions can be our psyche's way of calling attention to unhelpful beliefs and illusions that no longer serve us. If the situation felt familiar, try to get a bead on why—what does it remind you of?

When you've got the answer, express and release the emotion using the four steps, and imagine that you're releasing that old previously unconscious experience at the same time. Eventually, you'll notice that the triggers don't have as great an effect on you—and then you can congratulate yourself on the fact that you're well along in the healing process!

Identifying your true self

This exercise can help you identify aspects of your authentic self, as well as qualities you may have adopted from your parents or caregivers that don't fit who you really are inside.

1. List ten characteristics that you feel describe the "real you," such as loving, helpful, giving, needy, introspective, changeable, organized, etc.

2. Take a moment to tune in to your center. Close your eyes, breathe deeply for a moment, and focus on your heart. Pull all of your energy into yourself so that the outside world goes away for a few moments.

3. Open your eyes. Go back over the list and see which of those characteristics feel like who you truly are, and which feel like you might have taken on from someone else or developed in order to keep yourself safe from criticism. Circle those qualities, and look at what's left.

4. Do any of the characteristics left on the page clearly describe a parental or authority figure in your life—someone who might have "dumped" some of their own emotional baggage on you? Cross those off, and look at what's left.

5. Close your eyes again, and imagine meeting your soul face to face. What is your soul like? Does he or she look like you, or look different? How does your soul interact with you? Take as long as you want to be with your soul, asking questions if you like, or receiving advice.

6. Open your eyes and go back to your list. Are there any characteristics you'd like to add that you feel describe who you are in your heart and soul?

Identifying your personal values

Another way to connect with a deeper part of yourself and ferret out the negative messages you might have received is to complete a values survey. The values your parents held may not be important to you; in fact, you may value other aspects of life much more.

Perhaps your parents valued money and security above everything else (this was true for many people who grew up during the Depression). But you might value supportive friendships, creativity, or self-expression more than money and security.

It's perfectly okay to value different things than your parents did. In fact, it's part of what makes you uniquely you, and values often change over time as our society changes.

Every soul comes into the world with a purpose, and by discovering what you value, you move closer to an authentic expression of who you really are and increase the likelihood that you'll be able to reach the potential you were meant to attain in this life.

Divide a page of your journal into four columns, and label them across the top of the page with the following titles:

My parents' values	My values	Are values different?	Are values the same?

Using the inventory of values on the following pages, list all the values you think your parents held in the first column. In the second, list the things you value. Then check off in the third and fourth columns whether the values are the same or different. Keep the list handy for awhile, and let the insights you gain from it percolate through your mind and body.

Below is a list of values to get your started. You don't have to use all of them, only the ones that are meaningful for you. If you'd like to expand this exercise, you can search online for lists of core values.

Remember that each person is responsible for deciding on his or her own values, and each person has the right to decide what's important for him or her. Just because your parents had a particular value doesn't mean it's right for you—and it doesn't mean that their value is the only right one.

Abundance	Cleanliness	Devoutness
Acceptance	Comfort	Dignity
Accomplishment	Compassion	Diligence
Adventure	Contentment	Discipline
Affection	Continuity	Discovery
Ambition	Control	Diversity
Amusement	Creativity	Eagerness
Balance	Curiosity	Economy
Beauty	Daring	Ecstasy
Calmness	Deepness	Elegance
Camaraderie	Deference	Empathy
Carefulness	Delight	Encouragement
Challenge	Dependability	Endurance
Charity	Depth	Enjoyment
Clarity	Determination	Enthusiasm

Exhilaration	Intelligence	Persistence
Exploration	Intensity	Persuasiveness
Expressiveness	Intimacy	Philanthropy
Extravagance	Introversion	Piety
Extroversion	Intuition	Playfulness
Fairness	Inventiveness	Pleasure
Faith	Joy	Popularity
Fame	Justice	Practicality
Fascination	Kindness	Privacy
Fidelity	Learning	Professionalism
Fitness	Liberation	Prosperity
Flexibility	Liveliness	Prudence
Flow	Logic	Punctuality
Freedom	Love	Reason
Frugality	Loyalty	Recognition
Fun	Majesty	Recreation
Generosity	Mastery	Refinement
Gratitude	Meekness	Reflection
Growth	Mellowness	Relaxation
Happiness	Mindfulness	Reliability
Harmony	Moderation	Resilience
Health	Modesty	Resourcefulness
Helpfulness	Mysteriousness	Respect
Honesty	Neatness	Restraint
Humility	Nerve	Reverence
Humor	Obedience	Richness
Imagination	Open-mindedness	Sacredness
Impartiality	Optimism	Sacrifice
Independence	Opulence	Satisfaction
Industry	Organization	Security
Ingenuity	Originality	Self-control
Inspiration	Outrageousness	Selflessness
Instinctiveness	Passion	Self-realization
Integrity	Peacefulness	Sensitivity

Sensuality	Structure	Valor
Serenity	Success	Variety
Service	Support	Virtue
Silence	Thrift	Vision
Silliness	Tidiness	Vitality
Simplicity	Traditionalism	Warmth
Sincerity	Tranquility	Wealth
Solitude	Transcendence	Winning
Spirituality	Trust	Wisdom
Spontaneity	Trustworthiness	Wittiness
Stability	Truth	Wonder
Strength	Uniqueness	Zest

Dysfunctional families often have an "our-point-of-view-is-the-only-right-one" atmosphere, which leaves children with the feeling that others who have differing points of view are somehow wrong, and that they are wrong, too, if they think differently than others in the family. But there are as many value systems as there are people in the world, and all of them are appropriate in the eyes of the Creator. We were given free will when we were born, and it's up to us to exercise it, even if it means leaving behind the value system that our parents implanted in us.

How did your family influence your self-image?

Here is an exercise you can use to figure out how your self-image might have been influenced by your parents and other family members. Answer each question as honestly as you can. If an answer doesn't come right away, relax for a moment, and then check in with your stomach. Our bodies are great truth-tellers, and will usually respond with information if we're patient and truly want to know the truth.

Bear in mind that some of your responses to "I think I am" may be the same as your responses to "My parents think I am" because you have adopted thoughts and beliefs that your parents taught you, rather than developing your own based on your life experience. Others may be the same because that's who you really are.

Intelligence:
My parents think I'm _____
I think I am _____
I want to be _____

Money:
My parents think I'm _____
I think I am _____
I want to be _____

Work:
My parents think I'm _____
I think I am _____
I want to be _____

Relationships:
My parents think I'm _____
I think I am _____
I want to be _____

Self-Image:

My parents think I'm _____

I think I am _____

I want to be _____

Check to see if there are there any responses to "I think I am" that are similar to the "I want to be" response beneath it. Those responses would point to qualities that are part of your authentic self.

Your answers to "I want to be" will also give you signals pointing toward your authentic self. You can use these three questions to investigate any area of your life. Get as specific as you can with the questions and your answers.

Recommended Reading

The Highly Sensitive Person: How to Thrive When the World Overwhelms You by Elaine Aron

Finding Your Own North Star: Claiming the Life You Were Meant to Live by Martha Beck

Bradshaw on the Family by John Bradshaw

Healing the Shame that Binds You by John Bradshaw

Homecoming by John Bradshaw

Soul without Shame: A Guide to Liberating Yourself from the Judge Within by Byron Brown

Are You Really Too Sensitive? by Marcy Calhoun

Subtle Energy by William Collinge, Ph.D.

Warming the Stone Child: Abandonment and the Unmothered Child—a wonderful and supportive audio recording by Clarissa Pinkola Estés, Ph.D.

Mother Night—another great supportive audio recording by Clarissa Pinkola Estés, Ph.D. which will help you build your self-esteem no matter who you are or what you believe

Toxic Parents by Susan Forward

Creative Visualization by Shakti Gawain

Ask and It is Given by Abraham Hicks

The Dance of Anger by Harriet Goldhor Lerner

The Box of Daughter by Katherine Mayfield

Dysfunctional Families: The Truth Behind the Happy Family Façade by Katherine Mayfield

The Field by Lynne McTaggart

The Drama of the Gifted Child by Alice Miller

For Your Own Good by Alice Miller

If You Had Controlling Parents by Dan Neuharth, Ph.D.

Take Charge of Your Life: How Not to Be a Victim by Louis Proto

The Empowered Mind by Gini Graham Scott

Authentic Happiness by Martin Seligman

Learned Optimism by Martin Seligman

About the Author

A former actress who appeared Off-Broadway and on the daytime drama Guiding Light, Katherine Mayfield is the author of the award-winning memoir *The Box of Daughter*; a guide to recovery from bullying for teens and adults, called *Bullied: Why You Feel Bad Inside and What to Do About It*; a book of essays, *The Meandering Muse*; a book on writing memoir, *What's Your Story?*; a book of poetry; and several Kindle books on recovering from dysfunctional family dynamics. She has also published two books on the acting business, *Smart Actors, Foolish Choices* and *Acting A to Z*, with Back Stage Books. She has spoken at schools, libraries, and conventions on the subjects of recovery from bullying and creating an authentic life.

Ms. Mayfield's memoir *The Box of Daughter* won the Bronze Medal in the Reader's Favorite Book Awards, an Honorable Mention in the New England Book Festival, and was nominated as a Finalist in the Maine Literary Awards. *The Box of Daughter* was inspired by the title poem in her book of poems, *The Box of Daughter and Other Poems*. She blogs on dysfunctional families on her website, www.TheBoxofDaughter.com.

Websites:
www.TheBoxofDaughter.com
www.Katherine-Mayfield.com

Social Media:
Twitter: K_Mayfield
Facebook: KatherineMayfieldauthor